THE E
THE
An Adventure Series In Time,   Volume 1

Emerald

Falcon

Press

Published by Emerald Falcon Press
7386 Hazelcrest
Hazelwood MO, 63042
www.emeraldfalconpress.com

© Copyright 2004 by Deborah Solice.
Cover art © by Dave Barlow and owned by Emerald Falcon Press.
All rights reserved.
The Library of Congress has cataloged this edition.

ISBN: 1-933300-01-9
Printed in the United States of America.
This book is a work of fiction. Places, events, and situations in this story are purely fictional. Any resemblance to actual persons, living or dead, is coincidental
This book shall not be circulated without the publisher's prior consent in any form of binding or cover other than that which it is published.
No part of this book may be reproduced, stored in a retrieval system, or Transmitted by any means, electronic, mechanical, photocopying, recording, or otherwise without written permission from the author and publisher.

The Eye of the Undead

THE HIDDEN CHANNEL:

An Adventure Series In Time, Volume 1

By: Deborah Solice

This book is dedicated

In Memory of: My mother, Gloria Jones, for her excitement and for sharing the book with anyone who could read, and some who had to be read to!

And To: My daughters, Tiffany and Chelsea, for having the patience to put up with me sitting at the computer, day in and day out, and for believing in me.

Thank you to.
The Louisiana Reading Association for choosing my story as the First Place Winner in their annual *Educators as Authors* writing contest.

A <u>SPECIAL</u> thanks to all of my friends at Mansfield Elementary School 3-5 for encouraging me and for sharing this book with your students, I miss you all.

A sincere "thank you" to **Ricky Solice, Helen Jones and Jose Rodriguez** for all of the 'unsigned' illustrations in my book

A very BIG "Thank you" to all of my students at Mintz Elementary for contributing questions and your wonderful artwork.

Actual Egyptian Hieroglyph

Be young

Table of Contents

The Assignment 1

The Journey Begins 13

Surprise! 37

The Legend 45

The 'Guardian Cat' and the Mummy 50

An Innocent Mistake 58

The Journey Home 72

My Students' Corner 88

Guided Reading Questions: 95

        Picture of Osiris and Isis by Chelsea Solice.

The Assignment

"FINALLY! This must be the connecting corridor. If I can move fast enough to reach the opening to the secret passage before it closes, I just might make it to the next level and send the mummy back to the underworld. I wonder how many lives a mummy has any way? A cat has nine; but a mummy?" Tiffany was daydreaming about a computer game that she'd seen advertised.

The challenge of this particular game was to escape the clutches of an evil mummy inside an ancient pyramid, and send it back to the underworld before it takes over the real world. Players would have to elude the mummy from level to level. The lower the level, the closer to exiling it to the underworld. It was difficult to win because the mummy could appear, disappear, and then reappear without warning. Tiffany had been preoccupied with the game since the very first time she had seen the advertisement on television. During her daydreams she was adding elements that she assumed must be included in the game. She was obsessed with it, and was replaying it over and over and over again.

" ... and the first Egyptian pyramid was Imhotep's Step Pyramid located in Saqqara, Egypt. Imhotep built this pyramid as a tomb for King Djoser I. This particular pyramid wasn't just a tomb, but also a collection of temples, pavilions, corridors, chapels, halls, and storerooms. Three of Egypt's great pyramids are very well preserved and are also the largest pyramids. These were built at Giza. The largest of these is called the 'Great Pyramid.' It was built for the pharaoh Khufu."..... Ms. Bellard's lecture was droning on and on and on. Tiffany just couldn't keep her mind on the lesson.

She was twisting her long, dark hair around her finger as she was envisioning being chased by a mummy. Her eyebrows were scrunched together as she continued this imaginative plight through the pyramid. Ms. Bellard was Tiffany's favorite teacher, but Social Studies just couldn't hold her interest. So, as usual, Tiffany's mind drifted off to somewhere she'd much rather be. Of course, this particular daydream was fueled by the fact that Daniel had a brand new

computer.

Daniel was Tiffany's very best friend in the world and also her next-door neighbor. He was a few months older than Tiffany and had just celebrated his twelfth birthday. His brilliant, but eccentric, Uncle Ignacio had given him a new computer programmed with special educational windows that his uncle had designed himself. Tiffany glanced across the classroom and noticed that Daniel was also daydreaming.

His dark eyes were looking toward Ms. Bellard, but Tiffany could tell that they weren't focused on their teacher. She rolled her pencil off her desk and onto the floor to get his attention. It worked! The clattering got almost everyone's attention. Daniel glanced in Tiffany's direction and they smiled at one another. Each one knew the other was thinking about that new computer and how they wanted this class to end so that they could race home to do their homework and eat dinner, so they could check out the new computer games. The educational windows were programmed into his computer with admirable intentions, but the games would be awesome!

"... and don't forget that your research

assignments are due on Friday! No exceptions! A – N – D, I want you all to remember that this is not a '*mummy*' project. I intend for each of you to learn more about ancient Egypt than just mummification!" RRRiiinnnggg! The bell awakened everyone, and they all filed out to go home.

Tiffany began daydreaming again as soon as she

reached for her backpack and raced for the door. She never even noticed that she was weaving in and out of the 'sidewalk traffic' as if something or someone was in hot pursuit. The purposeful expression on her face was down right comical. Daniel spotted Tiffany scurrying down the sidewalk a few people in front of him.

"Hey, Tiffany!" It was Daniel. She had completely forgotten to wait for him.

He was so excited! He was grinning from ear to ear. Tiffany had been so eager to get through the day, and to get to Daniel's, that she was practically running home. She slowed her pace and waited for Daniel to catch up to her.

"Daniel! When should I meet you tonight?"

"Come over right after you eat dinner, Okay? Oh- Hey, why don't I ask my mom if you can eat with us tonight? You know she always says yes." Tiffany usually relished the thought of sampling Daniel's mom's cooking. His family was of Hispanic heritage, and his mom made everything from scratch; tamales, tortillas, pico …..uhmmm! The wonderful smells permeated every nook and cranny throughout their house, and the food was always delicious.

"Sure. Thanks." Their houses were only a block behind the school, and as they arrived at Tiffany's front gate, Daniel stopped and waited for her to walk into her house before he continued up the sidewalk to his house.

Tiffany ran upstairs to put her things away. She stopped at the top of the stairs to peek into her brother, Austin's room. He was sitting at his homework desk, flipping through his video game collection while he was watching afternoon cartoons on his little television. Her brother was focusing so intently on his game collection and the cartoons, that he never even noticed her standing at his door. Tiffany smiled and strolled on down the hall to her room. She dropped her backpack on the floor next to her over-stuffed pink daybed as she heard the phone begin to ring. She was just flopping down on her bed when she heard her mom call.

"Tiff, Daniel is on the phone." Gosh, she would bet that Daniel could hear her mom calling up the stairs to her all the way from his house next door. Her mom was completely unaware of how loud she could be. Her laugh could be just as exuberant and loud! Tiffany sat up, reached over, and picked up the receiver of her gold princess phone.

"Okay, Mom! I've got it!" "Hello."

"Hey, Tiffany. Mom said you could come over about 5:30 for dinner. Is that okay with your mom?"

"Hang on. Mom, Daniel's mom asked if I can eat dinner over there tonight."

"That's good, sweetie, because your brother has soccer practice, your dad's at a dinner meeting and won't be in until later, and I will be gone. So, yes. That's fine." Tiffany rolled her eyes at her mom's long-drawn-out -response.

"She said yes. I'll be over soon."

"Great! I'll see you in a little while." Daniel was just as impatient as Tiffany. The waiting was ridiculously hard. She put down her receiver and rubbed her hands together in anticipation of playing the computer game that she had been dreaming about all day.

Daniel had promised Tiffany that he wouldn't turn on the computer until she was there. He was tempted, but was determined to keep his promise. He kept himself busy by doing all of his homework before dinner. Then, he went downstairs to help his mother finish dinner and set the table. His impatience resulted in the need for him to stay busy so that time would 'fly by'. Unfortunately, his mother reminded him of the Social Studies project that neither he nor Tiffany could get interested in beginning, much less completing.

"Daniel."

"Yes, mom." Daniel's mom was taking the food out of the oven as she spoke.

"Have you and Tiffany finished that Social Studies project on ancient Egypt yet?"

"Umm, No, ma'am. Not yet. Mom, its sooo boring. Why do teachers give us such boring assignments?" He

sounded so distressed and frustrated, but his mother's voice was firm in her response.

"Daniel, you know how I feel about that. It's an assignment, and you will do your best work. Is that clear?"

"Yes ma'am."

"I expect the two of you to get started on it right after dinner. Okay? You know that it will be a great relief when you finally finish this assignment." Daniel's mom eased the sternness in her voice with a smile. Her dark eyes danced when they smiled at you. Daniel couldn't help but to smile back at her. She was always so predictable. You would never have to wonder what a response from her might be to any question. It would always be the 'correct' response that would encourage you to do whatever the 'right thing' was to do. In a way, it was very comforting because she was always steady and stable. No gray, just answers in black and white.

"Okay. I know you are right. It's just getting started and interested that's so hard." Daniel sulked a while when he realized that Tiff would be upset about having to do research on the computer before they would be able to play games. Oh, well. It would be a real

relief to get it over with and put it all behind them.

Actual Egyptian Hieroglyph

Ankh Symbol of Life

The Journey Begins

Dinner was delicious, but Tiffany and Daniel were too anxious to enjoy the homemade tamales, charro beans, and spicy Spanish rice. Daniel's mother loved to cook, and normally there were no scraps for leftovers. Even Tiffany, who was a light eater, usually stuffed herself when she had dinner at Daniel's. Not tonight! She could only think about after dinner. The two of them rushed through dinner, chewing and swallowing, but tasting nothing. Daniel's little sister, Chelsea, rolled her eyes at the two of them. She was only nine and didn't understand why they were so excited over a computer. Chelsea and Austin were also very best friends.

Daniel and Tiffany were always letting the younger pair tag along with them to the movies. They also had a standing babysitting job every other weekend because their parents would go out together as well.

Tiffany and Daniel finished eating in record time

and asked to be excused. His parents looked at one another; his mother nodded an affirmation, and Daniel's father promptly excused them from the table. They were in such a hurry that they didn't catch his parents smiling at one another over their excitement, or Chelsea snickering behind her hand at what she considered to be a silly reason to leave the table in such a hurry.

As they reached the stairs, Daniel's mother called out to them," Daniel, remember what I said about your project?"

"Yes, ma'am." He relayed the message to Tiffany as they bounded up the stairs to the family's study.

The study was at the very end of the hall on the second floor. There were bookshelves, a desk, a stereo system, and now Daniel's computer, all housed in this well-designed, but brightly painted, little room. Tiffany didn't want to act disappointed, so she just smiled and agreed that they needed to get started with their project so that they could finish it by Friday. She didn't see how this one could possibly be one of their most outstanding projects because neither of them cared about researching ancient Egyptian history.

This particular assignment was to choose an ancient Egyptian topic to research and to illustrate or construct a model in detail. Daniel's uncle had set up an Internet account for him also as a birthday present. Daniel signed on and typed 'ancient Egypt' in the address window. There were lots of choices. Tiffany suggested that they open the topic -'Ancient Egyptian

Pyramids'. There were other choices too, like 'The Burial Places of the Pharaoh's' and 'The Lost Egyptian Art of Mummification'. But, they just wanted to check out pyramid information mainly.

"I really wish Ms. Bellard would have said that it was okay to research a mummy or mummification. But, I guess she's right. No one would have wanted to research anything else because nothing else is as fascinating." Daniel agreed and clicked on 'go' and a small pyramid with a very tiny caption appeared.

"This is weird for this to be so small that we can barely see it," Tiffany observed.

"Yeah, at school the pictures are much larger," Daniel, responded in a puzzled tone.

"Click on maximize and let's see what happens."

"Okay, that's a good idea." Daniel maximized the picture and caption. The picture was still way too small.

"Look, Daniel, click here where it says hide channels." Tiffany pointed to the middle on left-hand side of the computer screen. Daniel clicked there, and strangely enough another channel appeared simply entitled – History.

"I've never seen this happen before, Tiff. Have you?"

"No. At least I don't think so. Click on it and see what happens." Daniel did and many choices of time periods appeared on the screen. Daniel found 'Ancient Egypt' and clicked on it. Then, he chose 'pyramids' and clicked on it.

"Look! All that trouble and it's the same picture

that we started with." The details in the picture were still obscure, and they could not read the caption clearly either. This was beginning to be more frustrating than fun. Tiffany's exasperation was obvious as she reached over and seized the mouse right out of Daniel's hand.

"Here, let me have the mouse and try something." Daniel scooted his chair over and let Tiffany have control of the mouse. She went up to the toolbar and clicked on 'view'. The choices shown on the screen were 'zoom in' and 'zoom out'.

"Well, I guess 'zoom in' means a bigger view of the picture." Tiffany shrugged her shoulders and with a flick of her finger, clicked on 'zoom in'; and all of a sudden they both heard a deafening roaring in their ears and felt as if they were being sucked into a mighty whirlwind. They were instantly cloaked in complete and total darkness. The loud roaring sound made Tiffany want to cover her ears. It was painfully intense and reverberated all around them.

Tiffany reached out and screamed, "Daniel!" at the same time that she felt his hand grab her arm. Horrifying thoughts of drifting in this formidable darkness forever had just entered each of their minds

when all of a sudden, in what seemed like an instant, they felt as if they were thrown from the very center of the whirlwind.

There was an eerie, still silence surrounding them. Their eyes slowly began to adjust to the light and to focus on the scene that was before them.

The two stood frozen in fear. Neither realized how tightly they were clinging to one another. Daniel, finally, after what seemed like an eternity, straightened up, relaxed his grip, and took a deep breath.

He turned as he released this deep breath and asked, "Are you alright? Hey, Tiff, it's okay." Tiffany's face was ashen and she was almost in tears. She just shook her head and remained silent, too fearful to even utter a word.

Daniel didn't admit it, but he was just as frightened as Tiffany. They were both in a daze. The two were standing right in front of the entrance to what looked to be the pyramid they had seen on the computer screen. It looked like a giant stone building composed of steps with an enormous entrance. They were both wondering if they were dreaming, or could this possibly be real. Neither of them said a single word. They knew they were experiencing something either very extraordinary or terribly frightening.

Tiffany cleared her throat, found her voice and asked, "Daniel, do you have a clue where we are? Were you able to read the caption on your computer screen?" He wasn't certain if he could find his own voice to answer her. He just stared at the scene laid out before him.

"It does look just like that pyramid on the computer, doesn't it? Yes, I did read what I could of the caption. But, I know where we are because I remember that Ms. Bellard said that there was only one pyramid in Egypt that was shaped like steps. It is Imhotep's Step Pyramid in Saqqara, Egypt. It's supposed to be the very first pyramid built between 2700 B.C. and 2600 B.C." He surprised himself, as well as Tiffany, by remembering details from a lecture that he only partially focused upon. He could really just kick himself right now for not listening more closely. He strained his brain to remember the rest of the lecture.

"But this whole thing doesn't look quite finished. There were supposed to be temples, pavilions, chapels, and some storerooms around here too. Something is really strange. It looks so new."

Tiffany looked around observantly and said, "I think you're right. It looks like it's still under construction in some areas." There were wooden ladders with baskets filled with unidentifiable tools sitting on top of some of them and beside others.

She also noticed ropes hanging from pulley-like

machinery. Nothing looked terribly old or 'ancient'. It seemed odd that no one was around either selling souvenirs or conducting tours. It appeared to be deserted at this point in time.

"Daniel, what happened? Why are we here?" He could hear the anxiety in her voice, but he really didn't know what to say to her. He was avoiding looking directly into her frightened green eyes, as he glanced downward and realized that he was clutching his backpack in his hand. He must have grabbed it when he was reaching for something to hold on to as they were

sucked into the whirlwind. Tiffany looked down at her hand disbelievingly and held it up for Daniel to see.

"Look, I must have clutched this in my hand during - whatever happened." She handed Daniel the mouse from his computer. It was wet with sweat from her fear and also from the death grip that she had on it.

"It's okay. I grabbed onto my backpack when – whatever happened, happened, too." He took the mouse from her outstretched hand, wiped it dry on his shirttail, and calmly placed it into his backpack. He glanced up at her with calm assurance that he did not feel.

"I'll put it in here for safe-keeping. We'll connect it - uhh, later." He didn't really know if he would be able to connect it later, but he was certainly hoping that he could. Daniel zipped up his backpack and slid his arms through the straps. He turned to Tiffany with a determined look upon his face. His voice didn't sound quite as determined, but he was obviously trying to take control of their situation.

"Look Tiff, there is no way that we can possibly figure this out by standing here and hoping that someone will come and take us home," Daniel spoke as curiosity, and a degree of fascination, began to override

his fear. Daniel's family traveled a lot, but they'd never been anywhere that could compare to this place. The movie theater was the only place he'd ever seen anything this extraordinary. He took Tiffany's hand and led her through the massive, columned entrance of the pyramid.

The corridor was lit with fire-burning torches. They were awe-struck as they walked down the open corridor to a huge chamber. The shuffling of their feet and crackling of the torches were the only sounds to be heard. The first room, or chamber, that they entered was decorated with blue tiles and engraved pictures on all of the walls. What they were seeing in this room was beyond belief! Astonishment shone on both of their faces. Their audible gasps of amazement conveyed the awe that they both were feeling. After a moment, Tiffany couldn't help but to verbalize her disbelief at all that was on display in this room.

"Daniel, look. I never thought I'd ever see anything like this." Daniel was shaking his head also in disbelief at all they were seeing. They had entered an enormous room. Tiffany was circling the room, trying to take in all that she was seeing, while Daniel just stood in

the center of the chamber staring at the fabulous spectacle. There were lavish pieces of furniture, such as chairs, beds, lounges, stools, and a variety of household items and opulent jewels. Many of the items in the room looked as if they were made of real gold. There was a precious collection of odds and ends positioned all around the chamber. Tiffany made her way to a far corner that had no ornaments or pictures, just a big stone boulder that looked like a pedestal with a glass-like green rock perched on top of it.

"Look, Daniel! This rock is just sitting on top of this boulder over here. Isn't it strange?" Tiffany picked up the rock and was turning it over and over in her hand, inspecting it carefully.

"Whoever left this stuff probably just set it over there to get rid of it and forgot about it." Daniel was so unimpressed that he barely even glanced at the rock that Tiffany was referring to.

"Do you really think so?"

"Yeah, look at all of this," he waved his arm around at everything on that side of the chamber, "of course they did. This stuff is worth something. That's just a puny, dull, green rock."

"Well, if you really think so, then maybe it would be okay if I took it as a souvenir."

"Sure. Hand it to me and I'll put it in my backpack for you." Daniel took his backpack off and unzipped it. Tiffany willingly handed the green rock to him and he tucked it away for her. They were so enthralled with the chamber that neither one noticed that the floor surrounding the boulder began to crumble and dirt cracked and shifted downward from the walls behind the pedestal.

"We should go and explore some of the other rooms in here just in case we might uncover a clue as to why we are here and maybe even how we might get home." Daniel made this suggestion as he began to get excited at the possibilities of this adventure.

Tiffany followed Daniel out of the chamber and into the corridor. She wasn't quite as excited about this 'adventure' as Daniel certainly seemed to be. As they left that chamber, the walls and floor continued to crack, crumble, and actually separate. They were completely unaware of the wreckage because their backs were to the room as they headed down the corridor. They turned right and went down another corridor. It

was just like the other corridor. Just as they started down this one, Tiffany became unnerved as she thought that she felt the floor of the pyramid begin to move. She also thought she heard a far-off rumbling sound that resembled thunder. She spread her feet apart to balance herself and looked toward Daniel.

"Daniel, did you feel that? Did you hear anything?" She was whispering in apprehension.

"It felt as if the floor was, I don't know, shaking or moving or something." Daniel glanced behind him to see Tiffany standing with her tennis shoes planted firmly apart, unmoving. He shook his head as a crooked grin appeared upon his face.

"It was just your nerves and imagination, Tiff. I didn't feel a thing." She was a little disgruntled at his comment and his attitude of dismissal. She felt something! She snorted in frustration. She didn't want to whine, so she decided against making another comment. They walked on. Daniel then halted at the entryway to another chamber.

"Wow, look at this!" They couldn't have imagined a room any more impressive than the one they had already explored, but this one definitely was.

It was amazing! There were many, many more jewels, and the gold decorations were blinding! Tiffany immediately forgot how irritated she had been at Daniel's earlier response regarding what she thought she had felt and heard. All of her attention had been redirected to this magnificent room!

"Oh my goodness! This can't be all real, can it?" Tiffany eyes were now as big as saucers as she stood beside Daniel surveying the contents within this chamber. They were so dumbfounded that neither of them had actually stepped into the chamber yet.

"I think it probably is if this is the real Step Pyramid," Daniel answered in an unmistakably disbelieving tone. He took a few steps into the chamber. Tiffany followed him closely.

"Now I know that you were right about the green rock. I'm convinced that it had been put aside to throw away. I could never have imagined anything this beautiful." This room was also decorated in blue tiles and hieroglyphics were engraved on every wall, and even on the ceiling in this extravagant chamber. They were both intently studying the scene before them.

Then, without a hint of warning, the entire room

began quaking and lurching upward. Many of the jewels and furniture began to shudder and then shift and fall from where they had been placed. One wall began to crack and shift and then to open as if it were a door. Pieces of the ceiling began to crack and crumble, raining stone and rock down upon them. This time they both stood with their feet spread apart for balance, afraid to move. Daniel was fighting to continue to keep his balance when all of a sudden, a beautiful cat bolted towards him, startling him, which caused him to flounder and stagger backwards. The floor lunged upward again, and Daniel fell against a bulging, ornate fixture on the cracking wall. As he fell against the bulge, the wall completely opened up and Daniel plummeted to the ground. Tiffany forgot her fear, and ran over to him.

"Daniel, are you okay?" Concern and distress were causing Tiffany's voice to tremble.

Daniel stood up, brushed the dirt off his pants, and calmly said, "Yeah. Yeah, I really am. It shook me up, but I'm not hurt." He couldn't help but to feel a little embarrassed at a girl, even Tiffany, running to help him.

In his embarrassment, as he was avoiding looking

directly at her, he turned and spotted the place where the wall had opened. His feelings of discomfort immediately vanished. He now sounded rather perturbed.

"Tiff, was that a cat that caused to me lose my balance?"

"Yes, it was. It seemed either very scared or it was chasing after something. I'm not sure which, but it soared through the opening in the wall behind you." Tiffany walked toward the opening as she pointed in the direction in which the cat had disappeared.

Now that the shifting and swaying in the chamber stopped as suddenly as it started, Tiffany realized just how frightened she had been. She turned to Daniel with a look of sheer displeasure on her face.

"I told you that I felt the floor moving!" Her hands were now on her hips, and her face was flushed. She felt like stomping her feet in exasperation.

"Yes, I guess you did feel something. But, look at the wall. It's opened up." Daniel felt really horrible for disregarding her fears earlier.

"Daniel, I really don't think that I want to see what's behind there. Really. I know that I don't."

Tiffany backed away from the opening as she spoke.

"It wouldn't be opening if there wasn't a room of some kind back there. Come on. Let's see if it's just another room on the other side of this wall." Tiffany didn't say anything, but she was very hesitant to follow Daniel to the threshold of the new opening.

He was doing it again; ignoring her feelings, and he had just apologized! She followed him because she didn't want to be left alone. As they approached the opened wall, they both slowed down to cautiously peek around and to get a glimpse of whatever was on the other side. They were both afraid to see what might be beyond the wall, but took a look anyway. After realizing what was there, Daniel visibly relaxed his stance.

"Oh, look. It's a stairway. See, I told you there had to be something here for that wall to have opened that way." Daniel stepped up his pace and led the way down the rock staircase.

It spiraled downward at a very steep angle. There were lit torches all along walls here too, but it was darker than the other corridor and was causing Tiffany to feel very uneasy.

"I don't like this Daniel. We are going farther

down into the pyramid. What if it starts to rumble again?" Daniel just shook his head, gathered his resolve, and continued on down the stairway. It really was kind of creepy in here.

He wasn't about to give into all of these fears. He knew they had to continue on in order to find out what had happened to them and also to find a way home. Tiffany had a really eerie feeling as she descended the stairs. She looked around at the gray walls, and at the shadows being cast in this dimly lit corridor. Ohhh – this could not be good. She felt as if she was being closely watched and the hair on her arms was raised in apprehension as a cold chill ran through her. She shuffled a little closer to Daniel

Actual Egyptian Hieroglyph

Crocodile, Collect or Gather

Surprise!

The pair continued on through the dark, spiraling corridor that was the staircase. They came to another chamber as they reached the bottom. This one wasn't ornate like the other chambers; no lavish furniture or decorations. It had a strange, pungent odor too. It was almost like the smells in a hospital, but worse. The stench was actually beginning to make Tiffany feel a little queasy. The terrible heat, humidity, and stuffiness weren't helping the situation either. She decided against mentioning that since Daniel was disregarding her feelings anyway.

They stopped in unison when they heard a rattling sound coming from behind a stone slab in the center of the room. Tiffany's whisper was thunderous in the silence that filled the chamber.

"Daniel, do you hear that?" Daniel signaled for Tiffany to be quiet as he began to walk quietly towards the stone slab.

When he reached his destination, he peeked over the stone slab at the exact same time that a young boy popped up from behind it causing everyone to scream in surprise. No one moved a muscle. They stared at one another for an exceedingly prolonged moment. Tiffany was taking in and mentally storing every little detail.

The boy looked to be in his early teens. He was dressed in a long, white loincloth with a white collar lined with gold jewels around his neck. On his feet were funny-looking brownish sandals. They couldn't see his hair because he had a white strip of linen tied around his head. It looked similar to what a nun would wear on her head except it was solid white. His dress was a complete contrast to Tiffany and Daniel's jeans, shirts, and tennis shoes. Daniel was settling down and beginning to think with a clear head.

"Hello. Who are you?" Daniel stood patiently and waited for an answer. There was an awkward silence.

Feeling sympathy toward the dumbfounded boy, Tiffany chimed in, "Maybe he doesn't speak our language, Daniel."

She stepped a little closer, unconsciously wringing her hands together, and quietly stated, "My name is

Tiffany and this is Daniel. Do you understand me at all?" This time the boy responded to the question.

"Yes. I am called Amir. Why are the two of you here?" It was so strange. Daniel and Tiffany realized that they could understand what Amir was saying, but his lips weren't moving to his words. It was as if they were watching a foreign film that had voice-overs dubbed in English.

Amir was looking at them with a baffled expression on his face, so they knew that he was experiencing the same bewilderment. Daniel couldn't help but wonder if this phenomenon was similar to the way languages were understood before the Tower of Babel. It was bizarre, but kind of cool too. Daniel's attention was diverted back to reality when Amir finally replied to his initial question when Tiffany prompted him again.

"Amir, what are you doing here?"

"I have been exploring the pyramid. My father is a tomb builder and he has been working here. My mother sent me to bring his lunch to him. I decided to exit using the corridor and spend the afternoon investigating this pyramid instead of being very bored

with my household chores. I became frightened when the rumbling began and I ran and hid behind here." Amir gestured toward the stone slab.

"I haven't seen any of the workmen since the rumbling began. There seems to be no one about even though the quaking has stopped. It is very strange. There is always someone working here, day and night." Amir shrugged his shoulders and turned his attention back to the two young strangers.

" Now, what are the two of you doing here?"

Daniel decided to answer with the truth since Amir had been so forthcoming with his answer. "We truly don't know why we are here and..."

"Uhhhh, Amir." Tiffany interrupted before Daniel said too much. She was still very curious as to why they could all understand one another if this was truly Egypt. But, she decided against voicing this question aloud because it would surely only add to this confusion. She quickly continued.

"What is this room for? It's not like the other rooms, and it has a funny smell that I noticed only in here." Her intentional distraction worked for the moment. Amir began walking toward her as he began

his response. He wasn't as tall as Daniel, but his eyes were just as dark and perceptive.

"This place is called a 'House of Eternity', and it is to bury our royalty. This chamber is a place to prepare the dead for eternity." Daniel and Tiffany grimaced at the thought of preparing the dead. Tiffany began to picture movie scenes that showed dead bodies in morgues.

After a moment, she made a connection and said, "This is where they make mummies! Oooohhhhh!" Tiffany's face expressed her aversion to even the thought of preparing dead bodies.

"Yes, it is a very long process. Those who prepare our dead labor tirelessly for many, many days. It is indeed a tedious process which can take seventy days to complete." Amir's expression became very serious and matter-of-fact as he gave his explanation. It was obvious that he did not understand Tiffany's feelings toward this ritual performed by his people.

"Why?" Both Tiffany and Daniel were curious and really wanted to hear the answer to this question.

"It is very important to prepare our dead carefully because we must be ready for the afterlife."

Daniel and Tiff just looked at one another when Amir made reference to the 'afterlife'.

Daniel recovered quickly and shook his head to let Tiffany know that she shouldn't say anything about the future. They couldn't tell Amir that they were from thousands of years in the future, and as far as they knew, no mummy had ever come back to life and enjoyed its well-preserved body, gold, silver, servants, pets, or any of the other items put into these chambers for future comfort. It just didn't feel right to interfere and Amir exuded such pride when he spoke of his heritage and traditions. Telling him any of this could only cause him to feel greatly disappointed and disillusioned. They both realized that they would have to be very careful to avoid doing or saying anything that could effect or change the course of history or that could destroy Amir's pride and belief in these traditions.

Actual Egyptian Hieroglyph

Unite, sum up, A total

The Legend

Tiffany decided to change the subject because she thought discussing mummies was kind of disturbing, and so she asked Amir, "Can you tell us about the pictures on the walls and ceilings in the other chambers? If I remember correctly, they tell stories, right?" She really wanted to learn as much as possible about these 'future' historical artifacts.

Daniel's face mirrored Tiffany's curiosity. Amir was obviously enjoying the unusual attention the two were bestowing upon him and began to tell the story with heightened enthusiasm. He strolled around and around the room as he told this spellbinding tale.

"Yes, the pictures tell the story of King Osiris and Queen Isis. Osiris and Isis were beloved rulers of the earth." Amir was animated as he continued the telling of his story.

"However, all was not well. Osiris had a brother, Seth, who was very jealous of him because Seth's greatest desire was to rule the earth. Seth's jealousy ruled his head as well as his heart, and he grew so very angry that he finally murdered Osiris, his own brother, and cut his body into fourteen pieces. Then, he spread all the pieces across the Nile River in every direction. At Osiris' death, Seth's ambition was realized, as he became ruler of the earth.

However, Isis, in her terrible grief, searched for and found the pieces of her husband's body and bandaged them all back together with linen cloth. With the help of Anubis, the god of the afterlife, Osiris was brought back to life. He could not live on the earth as a man again, so he became god of the nether world, or underworld." Tiffany was surprised when she realized how close Amir's storyline was to the video game she had been playing over and over again in her head. AND- She thought she had changed the subject to something besides mummies! Amir was still explaining the significance of the pictures on the walls and ceilings and their story.

Isis

Osiris

"Anubis became the god of preservation and Isis became the *Protectress of the Dead*. Osiris and Isis had a son, Horus. Horus was devoted to his beloved parents and vowed revenge upon Seth after he murdered his father. Seth and Horus fought a long, drawn-out, bloody, and dreadful battle. During the course of this horrific battle, Horus lost his left eye. He did eventually avenge his father in this battle against Seth and then became the ruler of the earth.

Seth was sent to the underworld where it is said the he skulks about on the outer-most edge awaiting any opportunity to escape and regain control of our world. Horus' left eye is an important symbol to my people. It looks like a falcon's eye and is said to enable the dead to see again. The 'eye of Horus' is critical to the mummification process for this reason. Also, the jars, called canopic jars, that are used to store specific body parts during the time one is dead, are named for Horus' four sons.

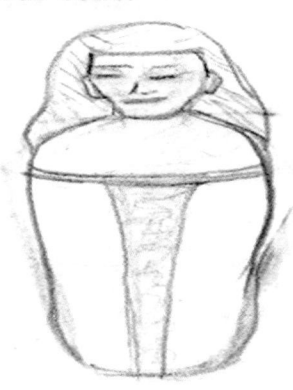

His sons were Imset, Ha'py, Duamutef, and Qebehsenuef. The jar of Imset has the head of a human and is to protect the liver. Ha'py has the head of a baboon and protects the lungs. Duamutef has the head of a jackal and protects the stomach. The last one is Qebehsenuef and it has the head of a falcon and protects the intestines. All of these items are used each time we prepare one of our people for burial. We believe a person must have a body that is still healthy and in good shape for the next life. So, that is the story of why my people believe it is necessary to prepare for life after death." Amir stood quietly, waiting for a response.

Actual Egyptian Hieroglyph

Army, Soldier

The Guardian Cat and the Mummy

"That was an awesome story Amir." Tiffany was really impressed. She thought that some of the tale was really grotesque, but fascinating none-the-less. "I've never given any thought as to why mummies were made in the first place, but I'm really glad that I asked." Daniel nodded in agreement. Amir's story was very interesting and enlightening considering that it explained the story depicted within the pictures on many of the walls in the other chambers.

Tiffany turned her attention back to Daniel and noticed that he was holding a funny –looking, long metal hook with a funny curved end in his hand.

He held it up for Amir to see and asked, "Hey, Amir, what is this for?"

Amir grinned and said, "Tiffany, I don't think you will want to hear my answer to Daniel's question." She just looked at him, placed a hand on her hip, and lifted her eyebrow as it to say, "Are you kidding?" and

shook her head yes.

"Okay. It is used to remove the brain from a person's body through his nostrils. One inserts this end of the"

"OOHHH! Amir, stop!" Tiffany quickly interrupted his explanation.

"You were right. That's more information than I want to know. Y-U-C-K!"

Daniel laughed and said, "I think it's kind of cool." Without warning, a blinding white light appeared, and the pyramid floor began moving and lurching up and down and the loud rumbling began, just as it all had before, but more violently this time.

The three grabbed onto the stone bed and held tightly. It felt as if they were riding on a roller coaster, but in a standing position, and without harnesses to secure them. Daniel felt something tugging on his backpack. He clutched a strap with one hand and held as tightly as he could to the stone slab with the other. The tugging became stronger and Daniel turned around to see what might be pulling on him with such force.

He froze. He thought he saw his life flashing before his eyes. Then, he was denying to himself that he

was really seeing what he was seeing. A being wrapped in white linens with an amulet that looked like the hieroglyph of Horus' eye around his neck, was standing there intently tugging on his backpack.

The light dimmed and Amir and Tiffany were looking toward Daniel and blinking their eyes rapidly. No one wanted to believe what they were seeing. This was just too insane. A mummy! No way! Oh, but it was, and it had a death grip on Daniel's backpack. Daniel was beginning to lose the battle for his backpack, when the cat that caused Daniel to fall into the wall, suddenly pounced upon the stone slab. In the next instant, the mummy simply vanished in a *whoosh* of air. All movement immediately ceased. The tremors and quaking stopped the moment that the mummy disappeared. Amir, although visibly shaken, was the first to find his voice.

"Something is terribly wrong. The amulet around that mummy's neck represents Horus' missing eye and identified the creature as Seth, Osiris' brother. Some believe that he waits at the edge of the underworld for a chance to rule the earth again. But, something in this world would have had to have gone terribly awry in order for that to happen." Daniel was as still as a statue, afraid to move and cause that mummy to return. Amir was in deep thought with a befuddled look upon his face.

Tiffany had to ask, "Why would Seth want Daniel's backpack? He wouldn't stop tugging on it, and the backpack was the *only* thing that he seemed to want." Amir thought for a moment before he responded to Tiffany's question.

"I don't have any idea why Daniel's backpack would be so important to him or even why he would appear here, at this particular time." The cat that had appeared as the mummy disappeared, was still sitting in the middle of the stone slab as if it were listening to their conversation. Tiffany didn't think that Daniel had even noticed the cat, much less recognized it. He was standing very still, staring into space in an unnatural silence. Tiffany looked at Amir and raised an eyebrow in question as to what that cat was doing here.

"Cats are very important in our religion. They are believed to protect us from many entities, especially the incredibly treacherous ones." Amir stroked the cats back as it purred contently while he replied to Tiffany's questioning glance. He noticed the change that came over Daniel the minute that he referred to this beautiful cat.

Daniel responded with a slight sneer, and the skepticism he felt regarding Amir's explanation was clearly evident.

"This cat is a menace! It caused me to fall into a wall that opened up and eventually landed us in here with that mummy. I doubt it was *protecting* me when that happened."

"No, you cannot believe that any cat would cause harm to befall you. I am certain that this cat was, in some way, helping you." Amir couldn't imagine this sacred cat creating havoc at any time. They were revered even in death. These creatures were the 'guardians' of his people. Tiffany was still truly disbelieving of what they thought they had seen. Amir could hear the incredulous tone in her voice when she asked her next question.

"Amir, why are we being visited by a 'guardian' cat and a mummy?" She couldn't help the shrill tone in her voice when she mentioned the mummy. His outward demeanor was very calm as he responded to Tiffany's question, but his actual response frightened her down to

her toes.

"I really can not imagine why these things are happening. Have you two done anything out of the ordinary? Have you moved anything from where it was placed? Or maybe, broken something in the pyramid?" They had both forgotten about the green rock. Daniel and Tiffany glanced at one another with looks of horrified shock on each of their faces as Daniel reached for his backpack, dug down deep, and pulled out the green rock.

Actual Egyptian Hieroglyph

Night, Darkness, Dusk

An Innocent Mistake

"This was on the top and center of another rather large stone pedestal. It didn't look important at all. The other jewels were definitely worth something in that first chamber, but this is just a green rock! Worthless! It just couldn't be of any importance." They both recognized the fear in Amir's eyes. They had been feeling the same way off and on through this entire, bizarre ordeal.

"We must find that chamber and put that rock back upon the very same pedestal from which it was taken. Anything that the priests put in this pyramid has a place as well as a purpose. I do not know what the purpose of that rock is, but I do know that nothing can be moved because it will cause a catastrophic reaction from the underworld." Neither Tiffany nor Daniel wanted to hear that. Tiffany looked at Daniel and screwed up her face again as if she was going to cry. What was he going to do now? It was his idea for her to

keep the rock as a souvenir. He ran his fingers through his hair in frustration as he tried to sound reassuring.

"Tiff, we'll just find the first chamber at the entrance to the pyramid and put it back. We took a rock from its intended place. That's all we did and it can easily be returned. Just take a deep breath. This is all my fault for suggesting that you could keep that rock. We're going to find the chamber now. Okay?" She gave him a slight smile and with the nod of her head, turned around to find an exit.

She realized that the 'guardian' cat had disappeared again. Tiffany didn't really care for cats, but this cat was really beautiful. It was solid white except for the gray tips on its ears and paws. She noticed its gray-green eyes immediately. It stood as if it were royalty, looking down its nose at the three of them. She wondered to whom the cat might belong. It was obviously well kept, and well fed. It surely wasn't a stray cat at all.

The three or them trudged back to the top of the rock staircase together, and were forced to stop at the first step. The opening in the wall was no longer open! Without a word being spoken, Amir's shoulders

slumped as he turned and walked directly back to the bottom of the staircase. Tiffany and Daniel followed him closely. They all spotted the entrance to the lower chamber at the same time. It was still open! A collective sigh of relief could be heard in the otherwise silent chamber.

"We will have to go the way I came into the pyramid and then find another way to the main entrance chamber." Amir's firm announcement offered a glimmer of hope to the otherwise daunting situation.

"We will follow you, but exactly how did you come to be in this chamber?" Daniel had only just this moment thought to ask that question.

"My father was building a storeroom on this level. If we can find that storeroom, we will find another staircase. I have seen it." Amir was *not* going to tell them that he was running to find a safe place when the rumbling began and he didn't even remember from which direction he had come.

The three began walking swiftly down the corridor. They really wanted to run, but then fear would take over and panic would consume them. As they entered the first chamber that they came to, another

flash of white light appeared and rumbling in the floors and walls began. This time they knew to be very frightened. They dove as one behind a golden bed in a corner of the room. They didn't even dare to breathe. They could hear shuffling over by the entrance. It came closer…. closer. They squeezed together as tightly as possible. Tiffany was holding onto Daniel with a fierceness she didn't know she possessed. She was sandwiched between Amir and Daniel and didn't mind at all even though she normally was very claustrophobic.

The shuffling sounded as if it were on the other side of the bed. Daniel felt a sinister presence nearby and peeked over his shoulder to see the mummy reaching once again for his backpack. He really wanted to just hand it over, but instead, he grabbed Tiffany's hand and pulled her with him as he flew around the other side of the bed and headed for the chamber entrance. Amir was right on their heels. They looked back as they neared the entrance. There was no sign of the mummy standing there. They didn't dare slow down yet. They turned around, back toward the chamber's entrance still running as fast as they possibly could, and

slammed into what felt like a brick wall.

It was Seth. There was a domino effect. Daniel fell, taking Tiffany down with him. Then, Amir tripped over the two of them and fell on top of Daniel. Amir felt himself being lifted into the air and roughly dropped on the floor beside Tiffany. The mummy was reaching for Daniel as Tiffany jumped to her feet and gave it a big push with all the strength she possessed. The wind was audibly knocked from her chest as she collided with him. It buckled her knees. He didn't budge. Amir was just getting to his feet, as was Daniel, as they witnessed the mummy's hand swiftly rising in an attempt to knock Tiffany aside when the 'guardian' cat appeared once more. Tiffany braced herself for the blow, but the mummy's hand never reached her because he disappeared at the same instant that the cat reappeared.

Tiffany turned around to see Amir walking toward Daniel, concern for his new friend written on his face. Daniel was obviously very shaken by his experience.

"Daniel, maybe we should just leave your backpack here and find our way out." Amir looked shocked at Tiffany's suggestion.

"No, Tiffany. Do you not see that everything will change and that evil creature will rule the earth if we do not find the chamber and put the rock back in its place?" Daniel was more composed now and felt that he must agree with Amir.

"Amir is right, Tiff. We are responsible for all of this whether we meant to do it or not. We have to put the rock back in its place." She just shook her head. She wanted nothing more than to go home. She never appreciated her home more than she did at this moment.

"This was not the room that my father was

working in. We must hurry and find it. More openings will close and walls will crumble as long as Seth is trying to gain control of the earth once more." That statement spurred them on.

They really did begin to trot down the corridor instead of just walking swiftly. Their footfalls resounded through the eerie corridors as they twisted and turned from one to another. When they approached another enormous chamber, Amir just glanced inside and shook his head. They continued down the corridor. That was not the storeroom they were searching for.

Tiffany and Daniel had lost the desire to explore anymore of the chambers within the pyramid. Their desperation to locate the entrance chamber surpassed their curiosity at this point. This abandoned, now silent, tomb felt as if it were closing in on them. They passed two more rooms with barely perceptible nods from Amir and all began to feel quite desperate at this point.

Then, Daniel saw movement from the corner of his eye. It was the 'guardian' cat again, as Tiff referred to it. It was headed down a connecting corridor. Daniel remembered Amir's comment about cats being sacred and protecting his people. He had been disbelieving at

first, but was willing to try anything now, after all, the mummy seemed to vanish each time that this 'guardian' cat appeared.

"Amir. Tiff. Look. There's that cat again. Hurry! Let's follow it." There was absolutely no argument. The three were frantic to find the corridor that would lead them to a stairwell that would, in turn, lead them to the entrance chamber so that this madness could finally be stopped.

They raced down the corridor to catch up with the cat. It disappeared beyond an entrance to another room. This room was smaller than the others and only had a few shelves lining the walls. There were abandoned food scraps and tools littering the room. Amir shrieked in excitement. He turned toward them waving his hand in the air.

"This way! Come on! This is the room where my father was working."

"Quickly! Here is the staircase that I was telling you about." Tiffany and Daniel eagerly began to follow Amir through the chamber, and up the staircase. Before they could take more than a few steps, from out of nowhere came the bright light once more. The whole

pyramid felt as if it was shaking and cracking, and the rumbling noise was louder than ever. It was almost impossible for them to maintain balance as the violent shuddering became more and more intense.

"Hurry! Hold on to the wall and run!" Tiffany and Amir rushed up the stairs, shifting drunkenly from side to side, even though they couldn't see a thing.

When they reached the top and started to go through the entrance, Tiffany noticed that there was only the two of them. She squinted her eyes until they became somewhat adjusted and saw that Daniel hadn't run up the stairs with them. She bellowed down the stairwell and her voice ricocheted off the corridor walls.

"Daniel! Daniel! Where are you?"

"Run, Tiff. Don't stop. Run!" She did run. So did Amir. But, it wasn't through the upper entrance.

The two raced back down the stairs. Daniel was in a tug-of-war with the mummy again. The pair rushed the mummy in a courageous effort to topple him. Instead, he managed to take the straps to Daniel's backpack and dangle him in the air while trying to wrestle the backpack from Daniel's death grip.

Daniel was definitely more desperate than scared

at this point. He was kicking his feet toward Seth in an unwavering effort to possibly throw him off guard. Amir spotted a large stone in a corner and made a mad dash to pick it up. He held it in one hand and was relentlessly using it to beat on Seth's back. The whacking with the rock didn't phase the mummy at all. Tiffany decided to rush him again and wrapped her arms around his legs trying to find another way to topple him. She shoved and pushed and heaved with all of her might. She wrapped her legs around him too hoping the extra weight would have some effect on him. Nothing was working. This episode seemed to go on forever. The three were feeling very desperate as their efforts were proving to be completely ineffective.

    Daniel was losing his grip when, in a single instant, the light disappeared. He toppled to the ground with a thud, and so did Tiffany. Amir was standing with the rock in his hand poised to swing at the mummy once again. Their eyes adjusted to the light as they spotted the 'guardian' cat sitting on the bottom of the stairs just gazing up at them. Then, it relaxed its stance and began cleaning its fur as if nothing out of the ordinary had happened.

Tiffany blurted out, "Where have you been? That mummy almost got Daniel's backpack!" The cat straightened its spine, pivoted and pranced up the staircase as if to say, "Who are you to doubt me?" She ranted at the cat all the way to the top of the staircase.

The three continued to follow the cat down the corridors. It seemed to know exactly which corridor to follow. Even more amazing, was that it seemed to know that they were searching for a particular room. Since none of them knew where to find the chamber that they were searching for, they just followed the cat without any reservation at all. Tiffany was going to blister the cat's ears once more, but realized that it had vanished just as it had before.

They entered the chamber where the cat had left them standing. They walked through it and exited using an entrance on the other side. Amir was beginning to believe that this corridor was familiar to him. He looked around and was flooded with a feeling of profound relief. He motioned excitedly for the other two to join him. Tiffany and Daniel realized that Amir was really bursting with good news this time.

Actual Egyptian Hieroglyph

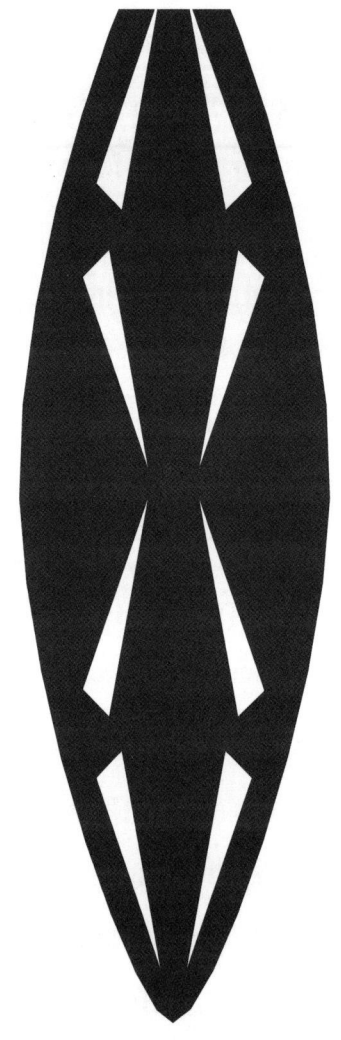

Bandage, Mummy, Cloth

The Journey Home

"This is it! It's the entrance corridor! I know that it is! Look! Around that corner is the tomb entrance, so your chamber should be there." Amir was pointing toward the far end of the corridor. He was so excited that his voice had risen to a shrill pitch.

Once again the three rushed to a chamber entrance. Daniel stopped and looked inside. It *was* their chamber, but it was wrecked! The floors and the walls were cracked. The furniture had fallen from where it had been placed. But, strangely enough, the pedestal was still intact in the far corner. Daniel put his backpack down and unzipped it. He began rummaging through it, looking for the green rock that had cursed them!

"Here Tiff. Hang on to the mouse so I don't leave it lying around." Daniel held the mouse up to her.

She took it and held it tightly with both hands. Daniel found the rock and took it from his backpack. It was really hard to believe that this little, green rock caused them to be in this predicament. He walked over to place it on the pedestal, all the while wishing he hadn't encouraged Tiffany to take it in the first place. As he was placing the rock on the pedestal, a hand seized his arm, ripping the cuff of his long-sleeved t-shirt, and knocking him backwards, away from the pedestal.

Tiffany yelled a warning and Amir ran to help Daniel. Seth had appeared without the bright, white light announcing his entrance. But, as the mummy began to reach for Daniel and the green rock once again, the 'guardian' cat appeared from out of nowhere and leapt on its arm. This time the mummy began to turn in circles and the sounds that were erupting from deep within him sounded excruciatingly painful. The rumbling and trembling in the pyramid made it feel as if it were on the verge of an explosion. Tiffany could feel the shockwaves running up and down the backs of her legs.

The movement spurred Daniel into action. He lunged through the air toward the pedestal and positioned the green rock in the very center of it. A

tremendously horrifying shriek of anger was emitted and faded into the distance as the mummy disappeared along with their 'guardian' cat.

In what seemed like slow motion, the walls and floors began to become restored. The rumbling had stopped. The room slowly began to look as it did the first time the two had entered it. Young eyes disbelievingly observed the amazing transformation-taking place all around them. Amir took a seat on a stone as he spoke to his two friends.

"We were successful. The threat from Seth is no longer imminent." He clapped his hands together in sheer relief.

The three friends smiled at one another triumphantly. They sat quietly for only a moment. There was no time to be idle. Daniel was ready to go home. He didn't take another moment to relax and savor their success. He stood up and wasted no time as he walked over near Tiffany and picked up his backpack once again. His intention was crystal clear to Amir and Tiffany. They were about to be on the move again, finding their way out and with any luck, home. The other two took the hint and stood, preparing to leave the chamber. Daniel had pulled the first strap in place when Tiffany began to speak.

"Daniel, do you think this is the reason we are

here?" Tiffany asked this question as she held the mouse up for him to see. Amir was watching them closely, trying to make sense of all that had occurred.

"I can not believe that just clicking this little mouse could have...." She clicked the mouse in an automatic gesture, and instantly felt the immense pull and heard the deafening roar of the whirlwind once more.

For a moment they felt as if time was standing still. Amir seemed to be fading away slowly. His mouth was moving rapidly, but no sounds could be heard. His hands were outstretched in their direction as he started toward them with a strange look upon his face. Then, the covering of darkness returned.

In the next moment, the two were standing in front of Daniel's computer looking at Imhotep's Step Pyramid on the screen. Daniel didn't blink. He reached over impulsively and grabbed the mouse from Tiffany's hand. He put it down onto the mouse pad, connected it, and clicked on 'close'. Then he exited and shut down the computer.

They both flopped down into the chairs that they had abandoned earlier. Neither of them budged for a few moments. They just sat there looking at the black screen recalling all they had just experienced. After a while, Tiffany calmly turned to Daniel and a comforting, lighthearted smirk appeared upon her face as she spoke.

"Oh my goodness, Daniel. I think we know more than enough to finish our research assignment. Don't you?" Daniel leaned back in his chair, crossed his arms,

and nodded to her in complete agreement.

They didn't mention Amir. It would be too sad at this happy moment. Of course they would eventually discuss what had happened and also remember Amir. Maybe they could someday find out if he exited the pyramid safely and what happened to him later in his life. It would be difficult to find out anything since they knew very little about his family and life outside of the stories that he told. But, they would certainly make the effort. It was just too somber a topic for them now.

They could only feel relief right at this moment, so the two friends laughed. They laughed until they could barely even breathe. It was the only way to deal with all the emotions they were feeling. The pair had experienced something that was unimaginable until now.

They sobered up for a moment and replayed what had happened in their heads. They were each so lost in thought that neither noticed the gray-green eyes peering out at them through the black computer screen, watching and maybe even waiting for another encounter. Then, they looked at one another and laughter erupted once again. Their uncontrollable

laughter echoed throughout the house.

Downstairs, Daniel's mother looked at his father and Chelsea and asked, "What in the world could be so funny?" They just grinned and shrugged, and continued to watch television.

Actual Egyptian Hieroglyph

Papyrus, Book

Author's Note:

Although the characters in this story are fictional, the Step Pyramid in Saqqara, Egypt is real. Many of the details and all of the history described in the story are true. The Step Pyramid was designed and built by Imhotep as a tomb for King Djoser I. Imhotep was the first pyramid builder. He also invented the carved stone, which was also used for writing. Many modern historians have uncovered evidence that leads them to believe that Imhotep was also the Biblical character that we know as Joseph. Almost every aspect of Imhotep and Joseph's lives were identical.

Although these details are factual, the descriptions of the chambers and hieroglyphs in this story come from many legends and stories found in the Step Pyramid, other pyramids, and ancient Egyptian artifacts. The story of Osiris and Isis also is a true 'Egyptian Myth', handed down from generation to generation. In some stories, Seth is referred to as Set. The story told here is only one of the versions of this popular tale. The details regarding the tools and jars used during the

mummification process are also as accurate as possible.

Tiffany and Daniel's next adventure takes them to 'Ancient Greece' and the original Olympics. Austin and Chelsea will join in on the adventure during the next saga.

ENJOY!

Deborah Solice

Actual Egyptian Hieroglyph

City, Town, Village

Glossary

abandon: to leave, desert

affirmation: confirmation

ambition: goal, desire

anxiety: worry, concern, fear

apprehension: nervousness, dread

artifact: object, work of art

ashen: pale, white as a sheet

audible: easy to hear, capable of being heard

avenge: punish, get even

aversion: dislike, distaste

awry: wrong, amiss

baffled: puzzled, confused

befuddled: bewildered, puzzled, confused

bewilderment: confusion, panic

bizarre: strange, weird, odd

caption: subtitle, header/footer

catastrophic: disastrous, terrible

claustrophobic: afraid to be closed in, fear of being closeted

cloaked: covered, shrouded

collide: crash, run into

corridor: hallway, passageway

consume: use up, devour

daunting: frightening, intimidating

dumbfounded: astonished, speechless

eerie: scary, creepy

exasperation: aggravation, annoyance

excruciatingly: unbearably, incredibly

flounder: struggle, move violently

formidable: alarming, frightening

gesture: sign, motion

glimmer: a gleam, a sparkle (in this story, a little bit of)

grotesque: ugly, gross

harness: strap

heritage: legacy, birthright

immense: huge, enormous

intentional: on purpose, deliberate

lavish: generous, extravagant

linen: cloth

lunge: thrust, swing

lurch: tilt, heave

obscure: difficult to understand, vague

obsessed: preoccupied, infatuated

ornate: elaborate, lavish, rich

pavilion: porch, gazebo

pedestal: stand, platform

perceptible: noticeable

perceptive: sensitive, observant

permeated: flood, fill, saturate

perturbed: agitated, troubled

pharaoh: king

plight: dilemma, difficulty

plummet: fall, plunge, tumble

profound: thoughtful, great, intense

pungent: strong, overpowering

puny: tiny, minor, small

pursuit: chase, follow

pyramid: a tomb for royalty

queasy: nauseous, sick

relentlessly: persistently, insistently

reservation: hesitation

resound: echo, boom

revenge: payback, to get even

ricocheted: echoed, resounded

ritual: custom, practice, tradition

seize: to take, grab

significance: importance

smirk: grin, sneer

somber: serious, sad

spectacle: display, scene

spiral: twisting, curving

stench: stink, terrible smell

threshold: entry, doorstep

transformation: change, conversion

unimpressed: uninterested, blasé

sulk: be in a bad mood, mope

Actual Egyptian Hieroglyph

Eat, Drink, Speak

My Students Corner

The following pages contain artwork and 'guided' reading questions submitted by many of my students as contributions to this completed work. All who participated put forth much time and effort. They did a magnificent job and added a touch of themselves to my book. Thank you to each and every one of you.

Enjoy
Deborah Solice

Actual Egyptian Hieroglyph

Sailing, To sail upstream

Derek Costa

"The Chamber"

Jamie Chapelle

Juatin Sapp

Chelsea Regan

Samantha Holsten

Katlynn Cunningham.

Cara Birch

Darian Riveria

Actual Egyptian Hieroglyph

Ask, Enquire

Honorable picture mentions to Natasha Rodriguez-Cosme

Guided Reading Questions:

1. Who gave Daniel his birthday present? *(submitted by She'Miaih Floyd, Matthew Barkley, and Tiffany Embden.)*

2. What was this present? *(submitted by Jean Acevedo and Jonathan Sanchez.)*

3. Describe the project that Daniel and Tiffany have to complete by Friday. *(submitted by Tyler Wallace, Chris Katros, and Logan Collins.)*

4. How did Daniel and Tiffany get into the computer in the first place? *(Submitted by Erin Berry and Bianca Lopez.)*

5. What does Daniel grab when he is sucked into the whirlwind? *(submitted by Natalia Claveria, Crystal John, and Brian Winfield.)*

5. Where are Tiffany and Daniel transported to? *(submitted by Michael Tourgee and Cody Maye)*

6. Retell the story of King Osiris and Queen Isis in your own words. *(submitted by Sabrina Zertuche, Sarah Martin, and Isaiah Bethelmy.)*

7. What kind of pyramid is Imhotep's pyramid ? *(submitted by Joey Ellis)*

8. What did Tiffany and Daniel take that had to be put back into its rightful place before Seth found it and escaped to rule the world again? *(Submitted by Justin Hartfiel.)*

9. Why was mummification important to the Egyptians? *(submitted by Lindsay Wallace , Chris Toney, and John Cazares.)*

10. Describe the canopic jars by telling which of Horus' sons' heads are on each, and what body part goes in which canopic jar. *(Submitted by Ashley Booker.)*

11. Who is Seth and what does he want with Daniel's backpack? *(submitted by Carlos Andino, Deryn McCoy, and Mark Simon.)*

12. What is the object that identifies the mummy as Seth? *(Submitted by Chris Herald.)*

13. How many times does Seth appear with the blinding light? (Submitted by Chase Haley.)

14. What unexpected creature helps the children to complete their task? *(submitted by Shanae Cole and Bre'Anna Jordan.)*

15. What were Tiffany, Daniel, and Amir searching for as they raced throughout the pyramid? *(Jesmar Colon and Paul Pucciarelli)*

16. Amir, Tiffany, and Daniel are obviously very different. But, tell how the children from the future, Tiffany and Daniel, and Amir, from the past, are alike. *(Submitted by Alek McKeever and Marissa Thompson.)*

17. What do you believe is the reason for the cat being there with the children? *(submitted by Alysia Cepeda, Leah McKinney, and Nieyshia Patrick.)*

18. How were they all saved? *(submitted by Owen Shaffer, Devin Baker, and Derek Costa.)*

19. What did Tiffany do that caused them to get sucked back into the whirlwind and into Daniel's family's study? *(submitted by Chelsea Reagan, Celeste Perez, and David Borges-Rivera.)*

20. What was peering at the two through the computer screen? *(submitted by Hayley Stepp, Heather Wilcox, and K.K. Bonner.)*

21. As you read about the 'gray-green' eyes peering at the children from the computer screen, write about why you think the cat is still there even though their adventure has ended. *(submitted by Ashley Parry)*

22. What was Daniel's family doing when Tiffany and Daniel were heard laughing from upstairs? *(Submitted by T. J. Ciesla.)*

Actual Egyptian Hieroglyph

Truth

About The Author

* Deborah Solice

* Resides: Temple Terrace, Florida with two daughters, Tiffany and Chelsea and their two cats, Felix and Clouseau

* Has been a teacher for twenty years, and a lover of books, as well as an avid reader.

* Began writing for instructional purposes and my students enjoyed the stories so much that I began expanding them for entertainment.

* This book won first place in the Louisiana Reading Association's 2003 – *'Educators as Authors'* statewide writing contest.

** It is the first in a series of books that takes young readers on adventures to 'real' historical places and gives them a sense of the history of our world through fictional characters and storylines.

*** Storyline: Two friends, Tiffany and Daniel, are hurled back in time through a computer program. They find themselves in a frightful predicament as they are trapped in Saqqara, Egypt, inside Imhotep's Step Pyramid. They meet a new friend, are protected by an extraordinary creature, and are pursued by an evil mummy that is trying to escape the underworld, all while they are desperately searching for a way out. Will the twosome ever escape this formidable tomb and find their way home?....

Actual Egyptian Hieroglyph

Look, Blink, Be wakeful

Look For These Other Books From Emerald Falcon Press.

THE NEXUS RIFT: What lurks in the shadows of twilight just at the edge of sight frightens us all but shadows that reach with sinister claws into the murky folds of time, space and dimension, well that would chill any ones soul. Come... travel with those haunted few trapped within this murky existence and wish them all the best... for they will need it.

THE SEEKERS: Come with us on a wondrous journey of discovery that will transport you to miraculous places on the globe, send you through the murky halls of time and with your help, guidance and courage save our earth.
   This book will educate you on volcanoes while it carries you through a marvelously told story, which stands on its own.

THE TOME of KNOWLEDGE: Have you ever bought your children coloring books? Well now you can give them something to color, keep and most of all learn from.
   Makes a great educational aid.

YOUNG HOPE: Young Hope is a very compelling story of how a family learns to adapt to the ever-changing brain dysfunction, known as early on-set Alzheimer's disease. A disease that is just now in the infancy of uncovering more about its mystery as technology begins to unfold and someday discover new treatments and maybe even a cure for Alzheimer's disease.

Look For These Other Books From Emerald Falcon Press.

THE TWONTLE: Come take a wondrous journey alongside a fantastical being as his mishap at the rivers edge sends him on a wondrous journey that will challenge his wit as well as his endurance. Written in a fantastic canto style rhythm that brings to life an interesting tale and lends one to an old fashion fable style of rhyme and rhythm. Remember those fables from when we were kids. Well this story will remind you and introduce your kids to this fun and memorable way of story telling.

FOT: A FATE FORESHADOWED: Enter a world of wild adventure, dangerous journeys, viscous creatures and wondrous terrain. FOT must regain the mystical stone in order to save his people and lands from utter destruction. This book is very well written with good characters and deep plots, you will defiantly enjoy it.

THE FORGOTTEN ARMORY: The moonlight glistened eerily on the weather worn black steel of the doors, which had stood for thousands of years against all forms of attack. Its thick chain links stood testament to its solid construction and its unrelenting desire to remain undisturbed. But here at this time, in this dark place you and your band have managed to open the legendary doors to the forgotten armory. Lying behind this vault like doors of hammered steel rests a gilded golden hoard of weapons never before seen by living eyes….. Until now...
This is a role-playing aid.

THE WAY to FAIRYLELAND: Follow a young girl on a journey through a perilous wilderness as she and her friends fight for survival. This adventure takes Lily on a wondrous ride into a strange world filled with bizarre creatures and dangerous situations.

LETTERHEADS and STATIONARY: We can make your favorite hobby, animal or whatever into your personal letterhead for your company or desk just let us know what you need.

BOOKMARKS: We have several unique designs from mountain scenes to fantasy artwork.

SCREENSAVERS: Don't forget to check our website for a very interesting screensavers. We have a unique screensaver for you. How would you like to have a living photo-album on your PC, simply look us up and check it out? We can put several digital photos of your choice together to make a unique and fantastic gift that fits anyone.

Actual Egyptian Hieroglyph

Weary, Weak, Tired, Faint

Don't forget to check out our website for the other exciting books and products we offer.

www.emeraldfalconpress.com

or our bookstore.

www.thewonderingsage.com

Buy direct for great savings.